A NEW YOU MAKEOVER

UPGRADING HUMAN POTENTIAL

BY JEWELS ARNES

INFINITE GOLD

COPYWRITE; SEPTEMBER@2019

Chapter 1

The Journey Begins

Infynite Gold High Frequency Skincare is the foundation of my heart. It is the voice of empowerment the wisdom of life. Yes, it is an all natural skincare line, but it holds within it the awareness of what it means to expand consciousness, the awakening of humanity! I believe we all have a choice in how we will take this journey through life. We can follow along having moments of knowing there is another way, or we can wake up in those moments and never go back. I woke up and choose to not go back. In choosing this, I became the creator of my life. Using ORMUS Elements everyday through Infynite Gold skincare, I enhance this Experience. ORMUS is a gateway to becoming conscious. It is a gift from the universe to all those who want to awaken and take back our birthright as the NEW human.

    Why skincare? The fountain of youth is attractive to us all. But why? Because society is obsessed with beauty? Maybe. The passion for eternal lift started long before the celebrities and models showed us what we 'should' look like. Life is also a choice, at least that is what was intended before unconsciousness flooded the minds of humanity. I believe if we truly use our minds we are capable of anything…. and I do mean ANYTHING! We can live without aging. It is a choice and I have dedicated myself to making a frequency based product that holds the intelligence of Eternal Life and the consciousness of 'Living' in this truth. I have dedicated my life to this truth, living my life beyond the beliefs or agreements of society. Living a life of choice is living an eternal life. It's not about being a supermodel, it's about being conscious. Choosing how we want to age is to choose to AWAKEN, choosing to be responsible for yourself and not to be a victim of life. Do I think I will live forever? I believe Eternal life is a state of consciousness and this it a pathway to achieving it. I am creating a higher blueprint that holds the gateway to Eternal Life. I will dedicate myself to the practice of awakening my consciousness so that I can become more and more aware of the choices I do have. These choices allow me to hold onto life force energy that I would otherwise lose 'unconsciously'. We can choose to die in awareness or live consciously, or die without 'knowing' we were ever alive.

We have choice in how we want to age. We age unconsciously because that is what has been done over and over. We have the power to age consciously and choose the path of our livelihood. The mind is more powerful than even the most advanced scientist can imaging! Let's tap in and live beyond our means. Living a life that is uncharted, beyond the programming of society, beyond what every other human has done before us. I dedicate my life to awakening my mind to possibilities most say is impossible. I take these impossibilities and give them to you inside a little bottle to use twice a day. This will give YOU the power to choose how you want to age, opening the gateway of your life beyond what you know in the now. This product has its own intelligence to assist you in reaching your highest potential!

Infynite Gold is skin care of the future. We are reprogramming our DNA to eternal life. Not by working with what has been broken, but by bringing the DNA to a higher level. This DNA is what I call an enhanced DNA program or Activated DNA. It is DNA living in the life force energy of the NEW Human or as I state in this journey, the NEW YOU. The NEW You, is a birthright we all inherited and it is the next stage of human evolution. Life is a choice. Aging is a disease. Let's claim our right to reprogram the DNA with our conscious decision…the decision to LIVE as the NEW Human. Live as the NEW You!

DIVE into Consciousness

A journey into the unconscious.

Creating with the NEW and upgrade your human potential

This is a program guiding you to let go of social agreements and bring your life to the next level! You will spend 3 days on each Exercise. You can use this journey as an anti-aging tool. It is an anti-aging tool of the future, right now! Spend time on each step and go deep. The deeper you go the more results you will see, feel, and experience!

Are you ready to take back control of your youthening process? Are you ready to Awaken to the highest version of you? Let's begin...

D: Determine- Can you commit to aging consciously? Is it something you can practice daily? Having a commitment to a mindfulness practice is a choice you make over and over! It's choosing to not be a victim of your life or how you "age" and become the creator of your reality!

Before you start this journey be sure you are ready to commit. It is a commitment you will make daily. This is not easy! You are changing the way you are wired. The stronger your commitment the more you will upgraded your human potential.

*Make a Commitment to a VISION of your Life From this Day Forward!

This is a practice of Awakening. A daily, life long practice.

Exercise:

1. Write out a commitment statement to yourself.

2. Why are you committing to upgrading your human potential?

What will your I AM statement be?

Every day you will use an Infynite Gold product of choice. While doing your skincare routine State Your I AM Statement aloud.

Place the product in your hand and rub.

Pat your face stating your I AM Statement.

Take a few moments to feel the energy shift as your I AM statement starts to reprogram your energy system.

Journal Page

Journal Page

Chapter 2

Is Aging a Disease of Consciousness

Using your mind to reverse aging, is using the conscious part of our brain we use to create an outcome. Aging is a disease. We have been conditioned to believe we must age or deteriorate and I these beliefs are not in alignment our current timeline; what it is to be human or the New You. Consciousness is the next stage in human evolution. We are becoming aware of the creator beings we are and taking this awareness to be the driver of our minds. Let's move out of being the victim of life… or letting the mind control us.

This is the evolution of humanity, bringing in the ability to not only be conscious of what we are creating externally, but also our internal existence: how we age. How we age is a choice. We can Become the manifestation of health and wellbeing with the practice of mindfulness. If we are made of energy, then we have the ability to manipulate this energy with our minds. You are already doing it! You are just using it unconsciously because of what you have been told through social agreements. We have been programed since we were babies, how we will age. How many times have you heard, "As you get older things just start shutting down."?
We have seen cancer disappear on a camera in less than an hour, seen things that medical science can't explain. Reversing aging is possible! You can be the creator of your own aging process. Sustaining and enhancing a

physical body of youth, is becoming aware of your thoughts and body and bringing them into harmony.

We can start living our lives in the frequency or thoughts that our body, mind and spirit is divinely intended to be... Because any disease, including aging, is the breakdown of a perfectly created vessel for our soul. We have the ability to live a life of awareness and reprogram the DNA to do what it is programed to do. There is an infinite source of life force energy within our physical body, holding information that will one day create longevity and vitality as a way of life, through a higher state of consciousness.

You can live within this state of consciousness with practice. It is our birthright to be the creator of our own youth. You can become conscious of your mind and body, allowing your cells to respond in pure love, diminishing disease, illness and aging as we know it! All that is needed is choice! Choosing new thoughts in each moment. New beliefs can be retrieved each time you perceive yourself as a creator. Are you controlling your mind or is your mind controlling you?

D: Dream- Claim your ability to reverse or create your own youth and vitality. Focus on accomplishing an outcome that is BIG! Pick smoothing you want to create as the NEW You. This outcome or manifestation will be used to break out of old programming so spend some time on what you want to create. Dream Big!

When moving through these next few days, challenge yourself to make choices from a higher frequency than where you are now. BECOME aware of how you are making choices!

Break out of old thought patterns that come up and bring your awareness to your back to you your dream. In order to create from your Highest Potential you must become aware of the negative patterns and create from choice.

Awareness and Choice is the pathway to upgrading your human potential.

AWARENESS TOOL:

Identify where you feel you do not have choice in your life. Is this true?

What would it feel like to change or except these areas of your life?

Try this!

Write about Dream and what it looks like. Paint your dream in your mind and write it down. How do you look, how do you feel? What kind of clothes are you wearing, what does your hair look like. Look at yourself in the mirror. How do you feel? See yourself as your highest potential right now. What do you see? Dream Big!!

Exercise: For the next 3 days

Take your Infynite Gold product and pump a small amount into your hands.

Rub them together and place them on your heart.

State aloud 3 times

"I AM connected to the Consciousness of Eternal Life, I am Eternal."

Close your eyes and say, "Show me."

In your minds eye SEE the codes of eternity activate in your body.

Now, open your eyes and say, "Thank you."

Journal Page

Journal Page

Chapter 3

The Alchemy of Infynite Gold: How it works

How does Infynite Gold High Frequency Skincare work? A scalar device programed with over 250 vibrational imprints starting with the God Particle. This frequency is used to bypass karma and spiritual law so that all other frequencies are not diminished and can be in their purest form without limitation. The scalar device is used to create a wave that contains imprinted information. Some of the frequencies used are HGH, repaired DNA, activated DNA, repaired telomeres, adult stem cells and other specific energies formulated to reverse aging. The frequencies create a full body balance working with the organs, hormones, endocrine system and the auric field, creating health and vitality for mind, body and spirit. The stored information can be within or outside of the dimension of the scalar wave.

Scalar waves are entirely different waves than Hertzian waves. The Scalar wave is a high frequency receiver and conductor used for accurate information that does not decay over time or distance. This energy performs with the energy system of the human body.

The imprinted energy is carried through a conductor, gold, and imprinted onto the ORMUS or M-state element substance. In this state, the ORMUS allows the imprinted energy to move in and out of the third dimension, bringing the imprinted energy into its purest form. At its purest form, life force energy can be retrieved and reconnected with the person of use. Each time the scalar imprinted ORMUS moves in and out of existence, more life force energy is brought back into the conductor or receiver of the gold, carrying the life force energy and other imprinted energy information.

The imprinted ORMUS then travels through the conductor, gold, by carrying the imprinted life force energy into the solid forms within the product, such as Shea Butter, coco-butter, and rose. The gold is used as a conductor of the imprinted energies, allowing the product to hold the frequencies at a higher frequency with the vibratory imprints of eternal life. The gold then penetrates the product ingredients deep into the skin, where it can work from the inside out creating health and wellbeing as well as the reverse aging of the skin.

The energies and elements work together continuously, gathering more and more life force energy. As they work together, they form the shape of a pyramid, collecting and creating eternal life within the God particle.

Infynite Gold isn't just a skin care line, it is a spiritual recipe of eternal life created beyond the third dimension.

D: Dive Deep- Think of something in your life you are struggling with? What was it? What feelings do you still have about it?

Bring this struggle to your awareness and notice how it is affecting your life or your thoughts and feelings in certain situations. Are you aware of the feelings and thoughts? As you go through your day become aware of fears and triggers that bring in strong or negative thoughts. Do you hold back or become small because you are afraid of failure or being humiliated? Humiliation and fear drain your life force energy. It's important to notice when your energy drops. Every time your energy drops today put a mark on a piece of paper or in the notes of your phone. If you have time, write down what happened and what emotion was the strongest… Fear of not being heard. Fear of not being excepted. Fear of bringing attention to myself. ect….

Exercise:

Before you go to bed:
Get your list from the day.
-Take an Infynite Gold product Elixir and put a small amount onto your hands and rub them together. Put your hands into a receiving position.
-Go through your list and recall the situations you felt your energy drop or when you were triggered.
-Put a picture, an object or a color to the first mark on your list in your minds eye. Send love from your heart to the object.
-Hold the object in love until you feel a shift in frequency.

-State Aloud: "I call back my life force energy with love and fill my cells with the light of eternal love."

Repeat this exercise with all the marks on your list.

Rest in the Love of the your Divine!

Journal Page

Journal Page

Chapter 4

Regeneration: Life Extension

Regeneration is a medical discipline focused on the practical reversal of the aging process. Regeneration is distinct from life extension.

Cellular regeneration is the bodies ability to recreate itself over and over. As we age declining levels of stem cells affect the skin's ability to remain elastic and repair environmental damage. Stem cells remain in the body throughout life. In fact, our bodies depend on these "adult" stem cells in order to keep us healthy and to repair damage of any kind such as from injury or illness. Adult stem cells are critical to health and disease prevention and it is depended on as one of the most important health discoveries of modern medicine. This discovery has created an age of stem cell therapy developments, including anti aging treatments.

Adult stem cells are created in bone marrow. The production of stem cells begins to decline as we age. When our levels of adult stem cells declines, damaged cells can be left un-repaired anywhere in or on the body, including the skin. The body will take the energy it has to repair the most vital organs in order to survive. That means repairing the effects of aging to the skin or hair will decline. At thirty-five years of age, stem cell release drops by forty-five percent, at fifty years of age, stem cell release drops by fifty percent and at sixty-five years of age, stem cell release drops by ninety percent! An infants stem cells circulate at 100%, by 65 years old these stem cells are only circulating at 10%.

Ormus mineral have been show to give the body the ability to regenerate Adult Stem cells as well as repair the DNA. Most expensive stem cell cream use stem cells of plants or animals. Why not give the body what it needs by introducing the intelligence to do just that! Regenerate! Ormus has been shown to partially reverse aging. When applied to the skin or taken internally over time the skin and hair are given the ability to regenerate because the rest of the body is able to regenerate with ease. Some effects of using Ormus Based skincare products are:

- A More Even Skin Tone
- Reduction of Age Spots
- Reduction of Fine Lines and Wrinkles

Infynite Gold is 'regeneration' in a bottle. It goes beyond healing the skin. It holds the frequency of healing the mind, body and spirit. It is skincare of the future today!

See the difference and feel the body regenerate from the inside out.

I: Imagine- Imagine yourself achieving your dream, imagine yourself as the NEW you. See yourself living a life of wellbeing. See yourself as a creation of youth and vitality. Create the feeling as well as the visualization. Play a movie in your mind achieving the highest level of youth and vitality and what a day would look like. Do you wake up and do yoga before having tea and watch the sunrise. Do you go dancing or hiking? Feel your body energized and full of life force energy. Keep the energy positive and exciting.

Did you know your mind can't tell the difference when a dream that is filled with emotion, and actually experiencing the dream? The same parts of your brain lights up and tells your body you are having this experience! The more you Imagine yourself as young and full of life, the more your body will rewire itself to this reality!

Imagine Imagine Imagine!!!!

Exercise: Go create your day! Pick one experience from your dream and bring it into your life today. If you can't go dancing, dance around the house. If there is nowhere to hike, take a long walk. Live your dream now!

Journal Page

Journal Page

Chapter 5

What is ORMUS and Why do you want it?

What is Ormus and Why do we want it on our skin (Transdermal)?

David Hudson patented ORMEs (Orbitally Rearranged Monatomic Elements) to describe a white powder, incapable of being perceived by the mind or senses, that comes from gold, platinum metals, and other "transitional" metals. These orbited rearranged minerals have not completely transitioned into the usual atomic structure or basic minerals. The electrons exist in a High Spin State. These elements come in and out of existence and can levitate! Being called the 5th dimensional element, they can become superconductive, and even resonate in other dimensions. Ormus Elements naturally exist within our bodies and in nature but with depleted soil and toxic lifestyles, we lack in these vital elements.

Ormus, also known as monatomic gold, white gold, white powder gold, M-state, and manna, is made through an alchemical process from water and other substances. It appears to be a phenomenon in all life-forms. It is matter in the monatomic state: a state between pure matter and pure energy. Ormus elements are being shown to be responsible for superconducting properties of all living organisms. Studies have shown that adding Ormus Elements to one's daily life, can partially repair the DNA, there for partially reverse the aging process. Reports of reduction of wrinkles, reversal of graying hair, increased metabolic rate and cell rejuvenation have been found.

Infynite Gold uses pure 24k gold and other intricate elements such as silica and brings them to a high-spin state, creating a rare Ormus element solution. These particles are left in tiny particle forms of less than 5 nanometers, giving them the ability to be absorbed to the basal level of the skin creating outstanding results. Ormus elements, are minerals appear to be directly associated with life-force energy, giving you the ability to slow down the aging process. Both gold and silica are completely non-toxic. Heating a monatomic substance raises its vibration level, which causes it to "jump" into higher dimensions. Infynite Gold makes Ormus Elements with extreme care and consciousness. Every product is consciously made and given specific energetic imprints that hold the frequency of reversing aging.

Putting Ormus Elements on your skin is like absorbing Life Force Energy, supporting life and vitality. Introducing monatomic elements to the skin, we cause a resonant vibration into the body where it is stimulated and harmonized. This "higher" vibration pattern allows not only our body to resonate at a higher vibration but also our minds. As we continue to add Ormus Elements to our body (transdermal), we begin to transformation our awareness of both past and future, beyond time and space into the experience of NOW. We are given a frequency to perceived everything with a higher state of knowledge and awareness. Where we were once a victim of circumstances, we open to a place of knowing and choice. Our intuition, mind and spirit, lead us into a life of wellness and longevity. The Ormus used in Infynite Gold can assist you in raising in consciousness! Support you in killing the virus and creating the disease called, aging.

Ormus Elements have been shown to repair the DNA. When we add Ormus to our daily routine, either through the Infynite Gold products or in another way, we are giving our body the intelligence needed to reduce aging as we know it. Ormus Elements Rejuvenate the body by giving the body life force energy that is lost as we age. It is literally telling the body how to reverse aging. Though it is new to our society, Ormus has been around since the Egyptian age. It is the food of the Gods. Now it is available to you….

"Rejuvenation is a medical discipline focused on the practical reversal of the aging process. Rejuvenation is distinct from life extension. Life extension strategies often study the causes of aging and try to oppose those causes in order to slow aging. Rejuvenation is the reversal of aging and thus requires a different strategy, namely repair of the damage that is associated with aging or replacement of damaged tissue with new tissue.

Rejuvenation can be a means of life extension, but most life extension strategies do not involve rejuvenation."

My personal experience with Ormus Transdermally:

When I started using Ormus elements on my skin I immediately saw my appearance turn back in years. I am almost 47 years old and I am told I look 35. Beyond the great results I am seeing with my skin, I feel the effects within my consciousness. I am more sensitive to my inner guidance and I truly feel the miracle inside this 5th dimensional substance. My health has improved and I am more grounded than I've ever been. Don't take my word for it though. This is something everyone should experience for themselves! Each one of us will have our own journey into what it means create longevity, it is a state of mind that brings us beyond the mind of the average person. I am done with being average... Being stuck in what I call Social Consciousness or 3D thinking. I'm living life in the UNSEEN. Beautiful skin is an amazing benefit! I love looking 10 years younger! But the true gift is the gift of Life in Awareness.... The Awakening of my Soul.

I: Investigate: Live from your dream today! Becoming the 'NEW' you. What thoughts do you have when you live in the mindset of youth and vitality? Can you keep a positive attitude? What feelings come up as you get ready in the morning, what do you pick to eat for breakfast or do with your free time? If negative feelings come up throughout your day how do you react? Feel? What did you say to yourself? Pay attention!

What does your body feel like? Are you tense and nervous? How is your energy? Are you gaining or losing energy when you experience different parts of your day? Why?

Exercise: Acknowledge throughout the day when you start to feel or think with the old 'you'. Break the pattern! Allow yourself to be uncomfortable not 'know' what to do or how to feel. Let yourself be in the unknown by not returning to your old thoughts and actions. Keep choosing to look forward.

For the Next 3 days write about 1 time you felt you were gaining energy and 1 time you were losing energy.

Try This!

You are made of energy, so life force energy is critical to your well-being. Life force energy allows you to experience life in fulfillment, without it you wouldn't even be alive. When you feel ungrounded, lethargic, depressed and uncertain, you are losing life force energy. When you integrate higher conscious and use intention, you bring in empowerment! This allows you to exist in higher states of mental and emotional energy that can revitalize your physical and subtle bodies.

Here are some ways you can bring back your life force energy:

Being out in nature

Eating healthy life giving foods

Sleep

Meditation

Breathe!

Exercise

Laugh!

Love others with compassion

What makes you feel full of life? Go do it!

Pick one of the above or choose another life giving exercise to do each day. It can be a 5 minute exercise... Just take some time to reconnect to the light within you and let it shine!!

Journal Page

Journal Page

Chapter 6

Killing the Virus

A virus is a thought or mental program we live by unconsciously or are only slightly aware that it is there. When we live by unconscious thought patterns we develop our reality through these patterns or viruses. The patterns expand out from our mind into our energy system and into the world as we see it through our own experience.

Aging is a disease. It is a thought pattern or virus that is validated as we age because we unconsciously adapt to a belief system of society, our parents, friends or teachers. What we witness as our 'reality' is being shown as we 'see' through the eyes that have created this reality. What if it is not the truth? What is an aging body is just a symptom of a belief system or virus? An unconscious choice humanity continues to choose?

How do we overcome a reality that has been passed down throughout the existence of mankind? By being conscious that it is an energetic pattern that, just like a virus, spreads into our reality. We have the ability to kill the virus by bringing it to the forefront of our minds and reprogram it into a more evolved energetic pattern. New energetic patterns are created when they repeatedly intercept old patterns. As unconscious thoughts begin to come into our awareness, we acknowledge them, witness them and then 'choose' not to agree with them any longer. Then we replace them with what I call an 'Upgrade'.

An upgrade is when we replace old dense energy patterns (viruses) that are beyond our understanding or a thought we have not had before. Something our minds cannot register because it hasn't experienced it yet… a reality that isn't in the reality of human kind! Our eyes cannot see it, our bodies cannot register it because our minds have not experienced it 'yet', BUT we ask for it anyways. We ask to be upgraded to the NEW Human. You ask to become the NEW YOU. A human that is not limited by the thought patterns of the humans before us. We create from the unknown, creating an unknown reality that is waiting for us to become conscious of!

We have everything we need to defy the law of aging. Let's challenge our minds and bring this awareness into our reality! When the programs or Viruses of society creep into your awareness proclaim your birth rite as a NEW You!

Be a consciousness advocate, push the bounds of what seems possible. Find your own interest around what it means to grow older. Most say we must inevitably grow older in appearance and decline in physical buoyancy... Start to question this outcome, decide today how you want to age!

V: VIRUS- What is your VIRUS? A VIRUS is a program that you live by without knowing it consciously. When you live unconsciously you have no control over your life, or the outcome. Pick one VIRUS you feel you get 'infected' by. It is an underlying feeling you have deep down inside and it usually is stronger when you are in stressful situations. When you are Creating the NEW You, though it is a positive thing, your body only registers it as change… and change is stressful.

Your body will not want you to change and viruses make it so that you feel, unconsciously or consciously, change isn't a good idea or needed. Change is hard because your body is chemically wired to resist it, to stay the way it is. Even if it is keeping you unhealthy, tired and unhappy. The body cannot tell if change is good or bad. It only registers it as stress and will release chemicals to resist it and these chemicals trigger our viruses.

Examples of Viruses:

I am not good enough

I will fail

I don't know what I'm doing

I'm not healthy enough to do what I want

I'm too old to play.

These are all viruses I took from CEO's of multi billion dollar companies! Even the most powerful people have viruses.

Exercise: Write down a few of your viruses and pick the one that has the most charge or affect on your happiness. Notice throughout the day when your virus interferes with your creation. Just notice it. Look it straight in the eye. Keep observing yourself as the virus comes up. Is it spreading? How does it feel? It is ok if you cannot stop the virus from spreading. What is important is that the virus doesn't become you. Just keep observing. You may still feel, act out and continue the pattern but you know you are doing it! This is the first step in breaking the pattern! The next time you see or feel your virus come up, observe again… keep observing. One day the virus will just lose its charge or affect on you and you will no longer be infected! You will be free of that virus and change starts to happen!

***Celebrate Every time you observe a Virus! You are Upgrading your Human Potential!

Journal Page

Journal Page

Chapter 7

What frequency is your life?

Living a life at high frequency is when we are aware of thoughts that are not in-line with our truth. If we live in awareness, we have choice. When I first started working as a vibrational therapist I instantly noticed a difference in how I felt. I felt connected and at peace with the world around me. Being around frequency work has opened my eyes to a world of vibration. I started studying what energy is and how it could change the lives of my clients.

After decades of working as a healer and deepening my own spiritual path, I have learned through experience and training, the art of Frequency.
So how does it work?
We are all made of energy; within our bodies we have places that energy is at high vibration, creating balance and health. Where there is illness, injury or depression there is a lack of energy creating a low vibration. In the physics realm, energy is a property of objects which can be transferred to other objects or converted into different forms.
So how can we use this understanding of energy to better ourselves?
If we are made of energy, then it is possible to convert or change our form using energy. All energy has a frequency

at which it vibrates. For instance, a magazine has particles that are very close together making it have more solid form or low frequency. The emotion of shame is in the

frequency of about 20 Hz. The emotion of peace is around 600Hz.

When our thoughts and emotions are surrounded with peace we vibrate at a high frequency. When we notice how some people seem to "glow" and others have a cloud around them, we are picking up their frequency. The higher the frequency, the better we will feel. The energy we are vibrating with is reflected into our daily life, our health, and our emotional well being.

When receiving higher frequencies, like through the Anti-Aging Elixir, your body will begin to resonate in this frequency as well and it shifts the energy of your body, mind and energy body.

With ORMUS intelligence it will bring low vibrational blocks, thought patterns and emotions into a higher frequency. We then become this higher frequency. When our energy body reaches a high vibrational state it will

remember what it is like to exist in that frequency and want to stay there.

In order for this to happen, our energy system will "clear" any lower vibration that cannot resonate with the higher frequency.

These blocks are what I call "programs". Most illnesses in the body start with a program; a thought or emotion connected to a story that plays out in the daily life. This can be conscious or unconscious. Clearing programs connected to anxiety, depression, anger or shame brings a life of choice.

What vibration do you want to live your life at?

We all have this choice and we all have the power to bring in the Divine energy to live a life of freedom!

Reprogramming the brain and emotional responses can be done with practice and awareness of when we have fallen into lower vibration (anxious, upset, angry, etc.) and choose to interrupt the negative pattern by seeing it for what it is... a program. A program is a story we have come to live by but is not the truth.

The higher vibration is always there for us to resonate with. We have the power by being aware of our thoughts and feelings, to choose our frequency. After all, we are energy and energy is always changing form. We have the choice to live a life of freedom and the world around us is a reflection of the frequency we are resonating with. Doing things that raise our vibration such as eating healthy, exercising, meditating, drinking high frequency water, or receiving healing therapies, will bring us to a higher frequency.

Try holding your favorite stones or carry one in your pocket and see the difference in how you feel that day. When I have a bad day I repeat "thank you, I love you" over and over again to the Universe.

These two phrases have a very high vibration and they can interrupt negative thoughts. The more we choose

things that feel good to our spirits, the higher our energy will vibrate.
What do you want to create with your energy?
If you resonate at a high vibration you will create a high frequency life!

Whether you realize it or not, you have energy that flows through you and extends to fields all around you. Scientist are now proving that you are energy! The new science also accepts that the universe, including us, is made up of energy, not matter.

Fields of energy around and with in you are forces that are measurable is an informational grid that is connecting you to all aspects of your health and wellbeing. The information stored in this grid or the energy connection you to all things is the foundation of energy healing.

Socrates said, "Energy, or soul, is separate from matter, and that the universe is made of energy – pure energy which was there before man and other material things like the earth came along."

Quantum physics says that as you go to the deeper workings of an atom, you will find that there is nothing there. It remains as just energy waves taking up space. It is said that an atom is actually an invisible force field, a kind of miniature tornado, which emits waves of electrical energy.

When using Scalar energy through an Elixir to improve health and wellbeing, you are receiving direct frequencies of the desired outcome. For example, if one suffering from a cold, the frequency of healthy blood cells and a strong immune system will be delivered to the person through a specific vibrational method, or in the case of Infynite Gold Skincare, through a cream or product applied to the skin. Many who have received energy treatments speak about the very high impact they feel they had on them.

Infynite Gold is created to vibrate above the frequency of 650 HZ though it is converted into Scalar energy. Scalar energy cannot diffuse over space and time so it never loses its frequency. It's more than just skin care... It is frequency care.

What frequency do you vibrate at?

V: Validate! Look for the evidence of your dream coming true! Focus on the positive and be grateful for every little sign that is validating it. What we focus on gets bigger. The more you see your creation of your dream coming to life, the faster and more you will achieve and receive.

Exercise:

1. Pick an I AM statement you can start to live by to replace your VIRUS.

Examples: I am an achiever

I am a perfect

I always do my best

I am Impeccable

I am lovable!

I AM the NEW ME!

2. Choose a small goal you want to accomplish today. Example: For the next 3 days when I look in the mirror I will see the beauty of my soul radiating through every pore of my body.

As you go through your day looking for the evidence of your goal and celebrate! Do you see yourself glowing? Do you have more energy? Do you 'feel' love in your heart just bursting at the seems? Do people want to stop and talk to you or do you receive an unexpected smile? Proclaim your light and let it shine!

When you become aware of a virus creeping in replace it with your I AM statement. Repeat it over and over until the virus has lost its charge.

Journal Page

Journal Page

Chapter 8

Breaking Victim Mentality

Awakening to Victim Mentality! Victim Mentality is "Anywhere you Take or Give away Life Force Energy in order to Feel "SAFE"

Are you the victim of your life/circumstances? This week is about Accountability and creating choice! You can't Ascend to a higher state of consciousness if you are blaming, dumbing it down, or trying to control. When I say

Victim Mentality, I want you to see it as resistance to life. The resistance can be seen as a coin. The coin has the resonance of resistance and empowerment, therefore holds both the same experience from different states of consciousness. Both are part of the same coin, but are being played out in opposite ways. So when you dive into identifying this pattern see it from both sides. Both are creating an energy pattern, one of resistance and one of flow. Victim Mentality is created anytime we "act out" of resistance to what life is showing us.

As you go through your week become aware of how you re-act to stress in your life! Do you blame the situation? Do you pretend there is nothing wrong? Do you try to control it or others so you feel 'OK' or in control? Upgrading your human potential isn't about having the perfect life… It's about identifying a frequency you hold that is resonating with the frequency of your experience. It is having awareness of what you are creating with your thoughts and vibrations.

Everyday write about an experience that you became aware that you were falling into blame, control or tuning out/shutting down (remember over doing is another way of tuning out)! Observe what other ways you avoid accountability or choice.

Make a list of ways you loose choice and become a victim or your mind or circumstances. This is the first step to having the ability to take action and use choice to change your life! It is important to know what your pattern is when playing out the Victim. Here is a list of ways the victim pattern can be played out:

*Blame: This is the Number one Victim Mentality

*over stimulating yourself or over doing in order to avoid a feeling or situation

*Bring others into conflict by needing to have someone on your side

*Repeating an experience verbally or mentally over and over without coming to a solution

*Control... Either the situation or people in the situation

*playing the poor me role

*Manipulation

*Bulling

*Passive aggressive behaviors

*Dumbing it down or pretending you don't understand when you do

*Shutting down or cutting yourself off

*Add to the List! Victim mentality is anything you do consciously or unconsciously that is giving away your power. It is allowing outside circumstances to have control over how you feel, act or re-act.

    When you identify the pattern feel it in your body. Where is the energy being held? Is it leaking, burning, building density? Is your heartbeat racing? Knowing when you are in a chemical response to a situation is key to ascension! It gives us choice in an experiences most react in. It takes practice to over-ride the bodies response to stress but being conscious beings, we always have this choice. It is a practice to be aware of the bodies response to stress. As we move into higher dimensions we will come up against these biological responses in other ways that can hold us back from achieving higher states of being. Learning to identify the responses, and the thought patterns that come with it is a huge step in moving past what I call the plateau or blanket. When you are saying to yourself, "I just can't get past this or I can't seem to change this not matter what I do. OR the big one, "I have been doing this work for 30 some years and I still am not too where I want to be."

V: Victim- See where you fall victim of your virus. Take back the POWER! When we are accountable for our thoughts, feelings and actions we have choice and empowerment. When we blame others for our thoughts, feelings and actions we lose our power to them and become a victim of our circumstances. It is always a choice to be accountable. After all we create our reality one way or the other. Where in your life do you lose your power? Is it a co-worker that gets under your skin? A relative you can't forgive? Your spouse or friend that just never understands?

Exercise: As you go throughout your day be aware of when you become a victim. Is it a car that cuts you off on your way to work or the store clerk that is rude for no reason? What thoughts come up? Do you blame, get angry or do you shut down? Start becoming aware of the story you tell yourself when you become the victim. Write out 1 experience either from today or from the past that you became the victim. Write out how you justified yourself and what you did?

Did you tell others your story so you would have someone 'on your side'?

Did you get angry and attack? Did you get quiet and sad until someone asked you what is wrong so you could tell your 'story' and get sympathy? Do you manipulate the other person into being wrong or bad? Become aware of your energy cycle so you can Awaken to the NEW you! Become aware of your victim patterns! You can't live a life of pure wellness and vitality, a life as the NEW you, when you are giving your energy away to your circumstances. When we give our energy away and become the victim we look for ways to get energy from other places. This cycle is seen everywhere in our lives if we really look at it. We get angry to take energy from the person we are angry at, we need someone on our side so we don't "feel alone". We stay quiet and sulk until someone pries the story out of us, we turn the story around and make others feel wrong or bad… these are all ways we unknowingly use to take energy from others because we have lost our energy to the circumstance that we became a victim of! We are just creating more victims! Break the cycle! Be the NEW You where you keep your power! No more victim, you are accountable for every part of your life. You have choice. Notice when you become the victim and see what cycle you gravitate to most. Awakening is change! Changing is the evolution of YOU.

Journal Page

Journal Page

Chapter 9

The Awakening: You have a Choice

Identifying the victim mentality is the first step to becoming conscious. Being unconscious is when we live life in a state of mind where life happens to us. We are pulled into the drama of life and get sucked down the rabbit hole of waking up in the morning, going to a job we hate but need to pay the bills, have health problem that we just deal with and we feel a deep disconnect to life… a feeling deep down that we are alone and have no control over our lives. The day we choose to no longer be a victim is the day we "Awaken". Yes we may fall victim to certain circumstances again, but once Awakened, we always will remember we are the creators of our lives. When we move out of the thought patterns of things are "done to us" and move into the thought pattern of "how can I bring this experience to a higher frequency and choose to release all resistance," we take back life force energy we lost through unconsciousness.

When we attract an experience it is the universe's way of showing us where we are vibrating. The universe has no judgement of where we are vibrating, it just gives us experiences that match our frequency. We judge the experience as good and bad because our minds want to control the situation in order to feel safe. What if we just noticed the experience as a lower frequency and choose to release it: let it flow right our of our reality? Resistance is the need to hold onto an experience. Resistance causes energetic blocks inside our bodies that cause us to recreate the experience over and over until it can be release. If it is not released, we first see it in our spiritual life. We feel lost, disconnected, lack in direction or clarity. Then we experience it in our emotions. We become depressed, have anxiety or focus on our problems. When we hold onto resistance we eventually will see it in our bodies as illness, injury or …. as a disease and AGING is a Disease!

Aging is losing life force energy. We lose life force energy when we resist life. Moving into higher states of consciousness is how we create longevity. You become so in tune with the universal flow there is no need to judge an experience. TRUST becomes your safe place. Let go of the need to control and allow yourself to be part of the natural flow of the universe.

When you experience resistance, use it as an opportunity to grow to an even higher state of conscious evolution. In this evolution you vibrate at a higher frequency and attract higher frequency experiences. Which includes an ageless life full of vitality! Your telomeres and DNA have their own intelligence. Your life experience can reprogram your DNA into a new evolution of what it means to be human! This is done by becoming conscious and letting go of resistance: maintaining life force energy! So jump into the FLOW and hold your hands high! Celebrate the good and the uncomfortable because it is all communication from the universe showing you where to LET GO and FLOW! Enjoy the ride of your own evolution! Enter the unknown and TRUST.

E: Exercise- Everyone gets stuck in negative emotion and self talk.

Choose ways to shift the energy! Using exercises to get you through tough mental, emotional or even physical responses to situations, helps you stay empowered and not fall victim to life, people or experiences. When you feel you are being charged or triggered, pull out an exercise. These exercises are used to break the chemical and mental programing your body goes into in stressful or emotional situations out of habit. In each situation you may notice you have similar feelings and reactions. You have the same fight about the same thing with your husband. You worry every month about your weight or health and think the same things and feel the same way each time. These are patterns your body is addicted too and recreates over and over because it's what it knows. Move into the unknown by breaking the circuit. Using these exercises or tools can interfere with those stubborn programs you live with consciously or unconsciously so that you can RE-create a healthier program as the NEW you… Start creating from the unknown instead of RE-creating what you have already done.

A box of tools:

Count from 5 to 1… 5 4 3 2 1 when you get to one you must "DO" something. It's telling your mind to get out of the lower part of the brain where we get stuck in emotion and negativity and bring it to the conscious part of the brain where we make choices!

Choose to be your I AM statement and "Do" something such as deep breathing, journaling, dance for 5 minutes, become the observer or "shake it off" with your hands. If all else fails start naming what you are experiencing. My heart rate is elevated, my hands are sweating, I feel sad and angry and it hurts in my heart, my breathing is shallow and it hurts to move. Naming what we are experiencing makes us more conscious of what is actually being experienced and keeps us away from being lost in the story and allowing the virus to take over.

Breathe! Take a deep breath and refocus. Focusing on the breath makes it hard to focus on your negative thoughts. This would be a great one to do when you are driving, working, or just out in public.

Reset! Tell yourself to RESET. Reset to your intention: Becoming the NEW you. Remind yourself it's okay to make a mistake, it's how you handle it that matters. Do you become the victim of your virus and spread it to others? or Do you use it to fuel your conscious choice to become the creator of your life! This is a choice you make over and over and over! RESET is telling your brain to not move into a habit or response and gives you the signal to consciously choose to d87o it different! New experiences are the way your body will change reactive responses! Remind yourself of your goal of youth and vitality.

Now come up with an exercise you think would work for you! Remember that an exercise is just that. You do it over and over just like learning a new sport or language. It is a practice of the mind. Just like a muscle, the more you do it the more it will work until it becomes natural. Training yourself to be the one that is in control of your mind is a lifelong commitment. It is the commitment that makes you either a Creator or a Victim. This is alway your choice!

Exercise: Practice using a few of these tools. Exercise them when you feel stuck or reactive. Write down how it felt. Did you learn something about yourself? How easy or hard was it to move into your empowerment? Did you discover a new virus?

Journal Page

Journal Page

Chapter 10

Elevate your Frequency, Elevate You

E: Elevate! Bring up the energy or vibration of your life. Like attracts like. Your life is a vibrational match of your thoughts, feelings and emotions! If your holding the frequency of failure, judgement or negativity you will create a negative outcome… you will spread your virus! This is the Universal Law. You create your reality by your feelings and thoughts. What feelings do you want to bring into your life as the NEW you? What VIBE do you want hold on a day to day basis? Elevate your VIBE by being the VIBE. Just like a VIRUS… Positivity and encouragement is contagious too!! No one learns or changes with negative feedback. It just make it harder for you to change. Be your best cheerleader! Instead of negative feedback when you fall back or make a mistake, try asking questions. What do I feel I did wrong? What can I learn from this? How can I improve or what can I do different the next time? We all have space to become better then what we are!

Exercise: Write out a time you lived out the reaction of OLD you. When you fell into negative thinking or got sucked into old mental patterns that left you feeling stuck. Now see yourself in the same experience and re-claim your power as the NEW! See yourself in the moment identifying and becoming conscious of the old patterns. Write out how you could have done it different. Awareness is Awakening! New experiences are the way your body will change reactive responses! Remind yourself of your goal of youth and vitality. Allow the NEW you to be there to make new choices when you are faced with thoughts that go against what you want to accomplish. Retrain the brain by believing in your goal. See yourself being young and free from societies beliefs on how you will age! Think it until you feel it. The brain cannot tell the difference between an actual experience and an imagined experience! When we imagination and feel a new experience in your mind, you are firing new responses just by thinking and feeling it is true!

Example: Be aware of old patterns and stop them in their tracks! I went to a do my morning meditation and noticed my back was hurting as I sat in my normal upright position. I noticed my mind say… "That's what happens as you get older, you can't keep up the way you once did." Then another thought came in that said, "I'm getting older, I can feel it in my bones." I feel my energy drop and I think, "Why even meditate?" Then the NEW me comes in and says, "Today I will recreate my youth and vitality! I may feel pain in my body but it is regenerating and healing in this moment! I proclaim my life as healthy and vibrant!" I see every cell in my body being filled with light and regenerating! I bring each cell into optimum health by celebrating and rejoicing the beauty of my body! It is a perfect creation of my Divine being. Today I chose to be the creator of my body's wellbeing by seeing it in it's healthiest form! I feel love for myself and meditate with the light of my soul as it grows brighter and brighter with each breathe.

Journal Page

Journal Page

Chapter 11

Living in Eternity

We are all more than we think we are. Our minds filter out what is conceived as "not useful" in every moment of our lives. We use only 10% of our brain. So much of our reality is unseen. Throughout history there have seen those that lived outside the physical world. This is still true today though more and more people are speaking up about the unseen world that exists: here, right now. Within this unseen world is a vast of information we all have available to us. In essence, it is an extension of ourselves.

A grid that holds frequencies and vibrations that attain knowledge, wisdom and a power that goes beyond the physical.

This grid is energy. The so called empty space between all things. This grid connects us all and it is within this grid we have the ability to truly experience ONENESS. If one were to see this grid with a seers eye, it would look like connective tissue. It connects all that is. It connects us to every dimension and goes beyond space and time. This grid is the foundation of life outside what is "seen". You are this grid. You are as big as the universe and as small as a grain of sand. Your body is part of the bigger whole, but also the whole in itself!

The grid is you and you are the grid. Moving beyond the limitation of the physical world is held in the knowledge that this energy is there and you have the ability to use it to expand your life beyond limiting beliefs, illnesses, thoughts, or anything that holds you back from being your fullest potential! The "unseen" world is where you can grow into the highest version of yourselves! Within this world you grow into a human that is capable of using the fullest extent of the brain. This is what you were born to be and this capability is just waiting dormant until you start being comfortable with exploring the "unseen"!

This energy grid of the unseen is a gateway to choosing life beyond what you know. It has no limitation and it can change humanity as we know it!

Let's explore the unseen and experience life beyond what is physical. Your physical makeup is just an energy pattern waiting to be "upgraded". Let's upgrade what it means to be human and experience life in the uncomfortable. Is it crazy to thing we can live an Eternal Life? I think it's crazy to repeat what has been done over and over… Humans evolve. The next step is to go where no man has gone. Let's change our world by changing ourselves, let's upgrade what it means to be human by allowing the "unseen" to be "seen".

E: Emerge and Execute! - Become AWARE of your thoughts and emotions in other areas of your life! If you noticed, most of these exercises talked about all areas of life not just around aging. Being aware of your thoughts and emotions in all areas of your life keeps you from losing energy. When you lose energy you lose your vitality!

Awareness gives you choice. Bring the practice of being a creator of the NEW you to all parts of your life. The more you "PRACTICE" being the creator of your life the more natural it will become and the more RESULTS you will witness! Keep finding the evidence of your Creation… your DREAM… the NEW you!

Exercise: Keep going! Make it a daily practice to notice when you fall into old thought patterns or emotional responses. Write them out as they come up. Even better… Start this program over! Keep going deeper! The more you awaken the more you create your highest potential. The more you live your life at your highest potential the more empowered you become. The more empowered you become the more you hold the vibration of living an eternal life! You have the ability to live in the consciousness of eternal life. What does that mean? It means you live as your highest potential in each moment. You live as ONE without resistance or old patterns. You become free!

Daily exercise: Write out one time you were able to notice an old pattern and break it. How did you do it? How did it feel? Be grateful! Celebrate yourself and the NEW you! Bring a soft pink light in through your heart and fill your body with joy and love. Today you took one step closer to being FREE. FREE from the way you used to think you would have to age, have to live… Today you Choose a new way. Today you choose the NEW you!

Infynite Gold skincare is a conscious product! Make it a mindfulness practice every morning and night by consciously applying it to your face, neck and decollate. First connect to your heart and feel love for yourself. Let this feeling turn to joy and smile at the beautiful being you are. Take each product and tell it what you want it to do. "I am regenerating every cell and reprogramming my DNA to the highest level available to me at this time. I am the perfect creation of my Divine self." Decide how you want to create your day. Do you want to focus on having more energy? Bringing in abundance? See yourself playing out the day and being in flow with the natural flow in each moment. Feel enthusiasm and excitement! See specific things you want to create and see them coming to be. Finish by looking at your self in the mirror and say, "Today I am the creator of my life. I create as the NEW me and I live outside the limitations of old belief systems I've put on myself and the belief systems of society. I am creating beyond the mind from a place of love and joy!"

Journal Page

Journal Page

Now go experience your day as the observer of your creation!

Become the NEW you!

Want more?

For more information or schedule a Face Reading and Private Session with Jewels please visit:

InfyniteGold.com

CPSIA information can be obtained
at www.ICGtesting.com
Printed in the USA
LVHW020717080623
749114LV00005B/217